The Lonely Years

Exploring Grief Through Poetry

The Lonely Years

Exploring Grief Through Poetry by

G. Greene

© 2025 G. Greene. All rights reserved.
This material may not be reproduced in any form, published,
reprinted, recorded, performed, broadcast,
rewritten, or redistributed without
the explicit permission of G. Greene.
All such actions are strictly prohibited by law.

Cover design by Shay Culligan
Cover image by G. Greene

ISBN: 978-1-63980-989-9

Kelsay Books
502 South 1040 East, A-119
American Fork, Utah 84003
Kelsaybooks.com

Acknowledgments

Thank you to the following publications, in which versions of these poems previously appeared:

Cable Street: "Clouds"
Eighth Annual Robert P. Collén Poetry Competition Compendium: "While I'm Sleeping" (2nd place)
Greenfield Recorder 30th Annual Poet's Seat Poetry Contest Compendium: "Day 348" (Finalist)
Greenfield Recorder 31st Annual Poet's Seat Poetry Contest Compendium: "Who's a Good Boy?" (Finalist)
The Montague Reporter: "Wish Fulfillment," "Coma," "Irreplaceable," "Existence," "My New Lover," "Upside," "The Greef," "Trees," "How Dare I?," "Clouds," "Hug Me"
Nine Mile Books & Literary Magazine: "While I'm Sleeping"
Rattle: "A Poem About Not Getting a Dog"
Witty Partition (now Cable Street): "Singular," "Serial Killer," "As Morning Approaches"

Contents

Who is this book for?
Dedication

While I'm Sleeping	19
Serial Killer	21
Day 348	23
Who's a Good Boy?	24
Clouds	26
Waffles and Chocolate	27
Existence	29
Coma	31
For Everyone Else	32
Preservation	33
Day Trip	35
Bottomless	36
Singular	37
not enough prednisone	38
A Poem About Not Getting a Dog	41
Dreams	43
Empathy for a Spider	44
Elephant in the Room	46
Butterscotch	48
Möbius Trip	49
Ghosts	50
The Greef	51
The Visitor	54
going under	55
Time Heals	56
Upside	57
Gravity	58
What Do You Get the Woman Who Has Nothing?	59
As Morning Approaches	60

Grumpy Dog	61
Winter	62
My New Lover	63
What Is This Place?	64
Half a Loaf	67
Trees	68
Race Point Beach	69
The Web We Weave	71
How Dare I?	72
Sunrise	74
Hug Me	75
If I'd Been Your Dog	76
I Am	77
If I Were a Dog	78
If I Had Been Your Cat	79
Smoke and Mirrors	80
Kiss It Better	81
My Ghost	82
Simple Pleasures	83
Sandy	84
Christmas 2021	86
No Upside	88
Salvation	89
Last Rites	91
Roommates	93
Ashes to Ashes	94
Reconciled	96
Dead End	98
Inside Voice	99
Piglets	100
Brainiac	101
Picture Perfect	102

In the Moment	105
Of Red Queens and Rabbit Holes	106
No Choice	107
Bent	108
Memento Mori	109
Leaving Home	110
Irreplaceable	111
Crossword	113
Ice	114
Ghost	116
Free Solo	117
What She Doesn't Understand	119
Enough Said	120
Next	121
Fixer	123
Customer Service	125
Photons	127
Obituary	128
Closure	129
Beyond Imagining	130
Sundays	131
Silence	133
Plane Crash	134
Appointed	135
The Problem	136
The Silence	138
Pyhhric Victory II	139
Rain	140
Sinner	141
What I Loved	142
Motive Force	143
Roll Credits	145

Vigil	146
Supernova	148
Epilogue	149

Who is this book for?

I think of this book as poetry with a purpose. That purpose is to offer anyone grieving the loss of someone they loved the opportunity to feel less alone, and a chance to see how someone else is navigating the terrain of grief. Perhaps they even get to see emotions they've been unable to put into words—put into words.

At the same time, it's not meant to be prescriptive. In other words, there are no "solutions" here or a suggested pathway out of one's grief—but there may be some catharsis for those who decide to read on. Much like talking with someone about one's grief can help relieve the pain, I believe that experiencing these pieces, written by someone who is grieving, may do the same.

Of course, it's also simply a book of poems. Now, I get it—poetry isn't an especially popular genre. But before you say, "I'm out. Poetry's not my thing," I'd ask you to think of these pages as just a collection of very short stories because most of them are based on real events and very real feelings. (For example, while the first poem, "While I'm Sleeping" may sound like a melancholy, made-up tale, it's not. For a time, I smoothed the velour of my wife's favorite chair before retiring each evening. Only later, when I understood why I was doing what I was doing, could I write about it.)

So, feel free to read these poems like little stories, versus reading them as poems. There's no need to fret about where the lines break or new stanzas begin because, in the end, none of that matters. There's no "wrong" way to read any of these poems. Ideally, there are a few pieces in this volume, hopefully more than a few, that will touch your heart; that you can relate to; that make you say, "That's how it feels!"—and discover it's a relief to know you're not alone with that feeling.

The Lonely Years is a follow-up to my first book, *Poems in a Time of Grief*. Though I'm proud of that book, I think this one is even better, if only because of long hours of practice and editing. Writing both of them has been the most effective way for me to process the loss of my spouse.

At the suggestion of a grief therapist, I assembled my early poems into the first book. They thought that such raw emotion might offer comfort, solace, and a sense of connection to people who shared my problem—the loss of someone far more important to me . . . than me. Based on reader feedback, it did exactly that. The writing didn't stop when the first book was complete, so now there's this companion volume.

So, what's the best way to read a book like this? The answer is, "In any way that works for you." You could read it in one sitting, front to back, in an hour and a half, give or take, but I don't think I'd recommend that. That's a lot of pain to take in in one sitting, and a lot of images to process. My suggestion would be to approach it in smaller "doses," a few pieces at a time.

You can also skip around and read pieces in random order. There's no plot to worry about and no building narrative, so you can read what follows in any order you like. The only goal, if you, too, are grieving, is that these pages allow you to examine and process your grief and what it feels like for you. Perhaps you'll even be inspired to pass this book along to someone you think it could help. If that were to happen, that's all I could ever hope for.

Thank you.

Dedication

This volume's dedicated to my beautiful, remarkable, irreplaceable wife, Jean Fielding.

In 2018, after six months of suffering, I lost Jeannie, my wife and partner of nearly forty years, to an undiagnosed autoimmune neurological disorder. I began writing shortly after her passing and in 2020 published *Poems in a Time of Grief,* chronicling my journey to that point.

As I write this, the seventh anniversary of my wife's death is approaching, and I hate that. I hate the fact that she's been gone so long. I hate living without her. I hate the notion that that number will only continue to grow as I live on.

The time that has passed since her death often feels like a physical distance between us, one that grows larger with each passing day. It feels abjectly impossible, yet I wake daily into a world where her absence is the central, abiding, and inalterable truth. She is my first and last thought each day. Her absence casts a pall over everything. I am deeply lonely, but only for her.

I share the feeling that many who are grieving feel, especially in the early days of grief, that there must be a mistake, that the world shouldn't be continuing on its course because the most important person in it is no longer alive. It feels as if the world should pause, at least for a while. But of course, it never does.

This makes the search for the meaning of, or the reason for, the death of a loved one maddening. The question of "Why?" reverberates around my wife's death for me and, in the end, is unanswerable. As unsatisfying, frustrating, and painful as it is . . . "Because, in the end, life requires death" may be the only answer available.

So, I continue to write these poems about my personal experience of loss and grief, living with grief, and in some ways, not living with grief. I write them because I am fairly compelled to. Once an idea occurs to me, I have little choice but to commit it to paper. I can't say writing them makes me feel significantly less sad, but they make me feel "explained," if that makes any sense. The writing of these works helps relieve an unnameable pressure in me.

As I continue to grieve my loss, these works are my salvation and my excuse, my thanks and my apology. They're a version of the love songs I wish I'd written when she was alive, not before she knew these things, because she knew how very much I loved her, but before I learned how to write them.

My wish for the poems in this book is the same as for those in the first volume. If you've known grief, or you're grieving now, I hope you recognize some of the feelings I've tried to express here and find solace in the words of one who has felt, who continues to feel, as you do. I hope you feel less alone.

—G. Greene

While I'm Sleeping

I imagine
that as I sleep at night
she may come to sit in her chair
or lie on her couch,
so I leave on a superstitious light
and ensure both are clear,
as there's nothing to be gained
by upsetting a ghost.

So my heart doesn't break
completely,
I made up a rule
and that is
she can't allow me to see her.
I haven't worked out why,
exactly,
but it must be true,
as I haven't.

I check for impressions
from time to time,
but there are only the marks
left by my own hand
where I've smoothed the velour,
which I do
to make it easier to see
some errant sign she might leave,

never on purpose,
as (another rule)
that's not allowed either,
but maybe,
one early morning,
a tear will slide down her cheek
unnoticed
as she hurries to depart
when she hears me
quietly coming down the stairs
and in her haste
a small, damp spot
will be admitted into evidence.

Serial Killer

Even serial killers do everyday things.
The serial part of serial killer
doesn't mean one right after the other.
It's not like serial killers
work an eight-hour serial killing shift
with a quota to meet,
or the boss asks them to work overtime
because one of the other serial killers called in sick
and the bodies aren't piling up.

No,
serial killers do their serial killing
between the routine stuff.
They get the groceries,
then kill somebody.
Restain the deck,
mow the lawn, maybe a nap—
then a little killing.
They take vacations
and when they return
there's killing to do
to get caught up.

But I'm not like
other serial killers.
I'm lucky that way.
I've no schedule to observe,
no master to serve.
I don't eat
or sleep
or get bored
or need a change.
I'm tireless,

relentless,
a prolific assassin of souls,
not bodies,
seeking my next living victim.
I am grief.

Day 348

December 14th will always be the day
Roald Amundsen bested Robert F. Scott
by reaching the South Pole first
and the date Eugene Cernan became
the last pedestrian on the moon (so far).

On day 348 of 1650
scullery maid Anne Greene,
unjustly presumed guilty of infanticide,
was hanged at Oxford Castle, England,
before being revived
at her dissection the next day,
to live on another nine years.

The Montgolfier's—remarquablement!—
tested the first unmanned balloon in 1782,
while a mere 158 years later,
plutonium was isolated.

Danish astronomer Tycho Brahe,
who would lose much of his nose
at twenty in a drunken duel over math,
was born on December 14th, 1546,
and just 472 years later, to the day,
you died.

I can just picture you,
first to arrive at your funeral,
radioactive with excitement,
embarking on your fresh adventure,
floating past the moon
with your new friend Anne
to join Tycho among the stars
and go nosing about the universe.

Who's a Good Boy?

Dogs.
Prized for their loyalty,
some so famous for this trait,
like Hachikō,
a Golden Brown Akita
who waited patiently
every day
at a Japanese train station
to greet his owner
returning from work,
for nine years,
nine months,
and fifteen days
after his owner's death,
until he died himself
on March 8, 1935,
that even now,
86 years later,
there's a statue at the station
to commemorate him.

No one thought to place Hachikō
on medication,
or suggest to him
that he move on,
or at least
consider a new owner.
No one recommended
therapy,
or getting out more,
or volunteer work,

or told him that his dead owner
would want him to be happy.
No.
Hachikō was admired
for his loyalty.
Woof.

Clouds

I woke in a cloud
cirrus or stratus
it makes no difference
but I can tell you
clouds are dark
on the inside

and hard to live in.
There's nowhere to sit
nowhere to hang a coat
and though they look
fluffy and cottony
they're soaking wet

and cold and clingy,
a flooded basement
in the sky
full of sodden memories.
I think clouds must be
made of tears.

Waffles and Chocolate

You expect the sadness,
tears,
guilt,
sleeplessness—
then the sleeping—
the depression,
all these a given.

But no one mentions
what lies in wait,
like a root arcing across
a darkened trail,
unavoidable;
wanting it not to be true,
wanting them back,
wanting whatever this is to end.

The want,
alive,
like some creature in your gut,
trapped, feral,
desperate to escape itself,
desperate for release,
freedom from this *now,*
this *constant knowing,*
all bared teeth and extended claws,
spittle and frothing,
tearing at itself
and everything surrounding it.

The wanting so terrible,
so complete,
so perfect,
that it's good
you don't have the means to indulge it,

the need to see, talk,
be with them,
hold them,
so thoughtlessly powerful
you'd send the universe back
to that first point of nothingness
to make it stop,
send it all hurtling back
with everything and everyone

it contains or ever contained,
send back the dinosaurs,
Einstein and physics,
the pyramids,
math, Bach, da Vinci,
the precious few saints
and all the sinners,
Kafka, Salinger,
mountains,
waffles and chocolate,
Poe and sunlight,
ice and Frost,
hummingbirds,
sex, stars, fog,
all of it,
everything,
in an instant,

if you could be with them
just for a moment,
cling to them
while it all collapses
into the reflection of how it began.

Existence

Composed of identical stuff,
wired to the same paradigm,
we are not,
nor could we ever be,
the same,
which is why
you cannot know my pain—
implying no failure
on your behalf
or mine.

Even if you have lived its circumstance,
that is your pain,
not mine.
You can no more grasp
what this horror is like for me
than I could know for you,
our agony,
composed of the same stuff
as ourselves,
never the same.

We cannot express its core,
share its gravity with one another,
living as it does
outside language.
We can only speak around it,
describe it in negative space.
I can tell you how happy we were,
you may share anecdotes of your life together,
neither more truly intimate,
more experiential,

than describing an electrocution
by explaining the physics of electricity.

This loss is an orgasm of pain,
blatantly universal
yet so stunningly personal,
fundamentally unshareable,
that even if
you've suffered passage
through this same gate
it opens to a different city
in a different world
from the one I occupy.

My city shrieks like yours,
your city screams like mine,
yet they are not the same.
We share so much
but we cannot share
the sensation of existence,
the one thing we truly have in common
and the insufferable divide
that finally separates us.

Coma

I awoke in Budapest
hungry for breastmilk
and the sound of children laughing

I awoke in Singapore
soul on the tip of my tongue
as courtesans bled the sky

I awoke in Rhodes
in a medieval fugue,
rats trenchant with plague

I awoke in Dubai
in the presence of Allah
texting an epiphany

I awoke in Savannah
in fear for the children
living in the eye of the storm

I awoke in Paris
drunk with the night,
talking to the Seine

I awoke in Calgary
frozen in a chalice of ancient snows,
feverish from the heat

I awoke in my bed,
more chaste than lead,
hungry for Budapest and
the sound of children laughing

For Everyone Else

For everyone else
two years,
four months,
two weeks
and two days.

For me
it was and remains
just a moment ago
I left the room
where your quieted body,
still warm,
no longer breathing,

begged me stay,
how can you leave me here,
what is this place?
You said you'd never leave me.
Liar.

For everyone else,
three Christmases,
two Thanksgivings,
the joy of remember when,
the promise of until then.

For me,
one long, long night
aches from darkness to light
to darkness again,
never a new day,
always and ever
the fourteenth of December,
and I'm leaving your room.

Preservation

I water your flowers,
keep your laptop updated,
bed made,
and the dishes are all done.

Your car is washed,
the patio swept clean,
everything the way you'd want it
ever since you left.

I keep the bed changed,
use those little sheets in the dryer.
The kitchen floor is mopped and
I try to keep things neat.

There's nothing in your chair
or on your couch.
Your clothes are waiting in the closet,
your shoes lined up beneath them,
just so.

You've probably lost track
but the ring they removed
is with the rest of your jewelry
in that little drawer,
the one in your bureau,
where you always kept it.

I still have what's left
of the last candy
I ever gave you,
your favorite,
white chocolate with almonds.

If I'm not here,
I'll be back very soon,
but it's in the freezer,
in a sandwich bag,
under the pot pie.

Day Trip

It's a hundred miles
to your favorite beach,
where the ocean
touches the sky,

only fifty
to the hospital
where your doctors
live with their lies.

Just six miles
to the nursing home
where the experts
consigned you to die

and barely five
to the cemetery
where my life
and your ashes
reside,

but ten thousand miles or more,
with cliffs on either side,
ere I ever reach the end
of this lonely, pointless ride.

Bottomless

No days anymore,
just dark
followed by light
then dark again,

no contrast, no calendar,
just dissent in the weather
to divide any dawn
one from another.

Time dissolved
as your life resolved
to each doubtful breath;
then one more.
(Please, honey—
just one more . . .)

Done so many times before,
it's unimaginable
that both our lives
simply ceased,
when,
after so many years,
you forgot how to breathe.

Singular

There are so many
hard parts
I'm not sure the plural
even applies.
Perhaps
the quietus of joy,
the crackling static of pain,
the sandpapered light,
your missing scent,
the fog of boredom,
the mummy's embrace of depression,
the silence
that rings off these walls,
perhaps all of these
are simply one thing now,
the after.

not enough prednisone

even in dying
you were one of a kind,
the way you went about it
confounding the doctors,
clues so obscure at first
we didn't know they were clues,
raising no alarm until
you reached a biological tipping point
where you collapsed
and were rushed to the hospital,

but even then
we didn't understand the gravity,
discharged by shrugging white coats
as you appeared to improve
but then failed to rebound
in the weeks at home,
new symptoms piling up
as we realized
this is bad.

the innumeracy,
the increasing struggle for words,
the stutter in your gait,
tenuous balance,
fabrications,
a fog of malaise
that made us insist they look again
and discovered
almost by accident
the fog in your brain,
lesions,

thousands of them,
hundreds of thousands,
suffusing the white matter,
marching down to your brain stem.

but the lesions weren't the enemy,
the lesions were the damage,
the damage that said,
"The enemy has taken this ground and moved on,"
so they searched in earnest now,
bleeding and cutting you,
sampling and assaying,
irradiating, scanning, electrifying,
always a step behind,
your adversary so cunning,
so adept,
they couldn't find it or name it,
far less treat it.

all the while,
as they went from hail Hippocrates
to Hail Marys,
your breathing became more difficult
by the tiniest increments,
just a bit each day,
requiring more and more steroids
to even make it possible,
as they struggled for a diagnosis,
groped for treatment, until,
shrugging once again,
your very presence intolerable,
their inadequacy smiling back at them,

greeting them warmly each day,
they sent you to a nursing home,
scheduling you for a follow-up
you'd never live to attend,
so blind to what was happening,
so unwilling to admit failure,
they were shocked when I said so.

so then it was "rehab"
in hell's seventh circle
where they did their best
to make you sicker
while denying your insurance,
as you struggled on against your old enemy
while I fought the new one,
and only one of us won their battle,

as there wasn't enough
prednisone in the world
to keep you breathing
as the secret of life was revealed to me
in the mystery of your quiet,
breathtaking death,
and the secret was—
you.

A Poem About Not Getting a Dog

I should get a dog,
unwitting but willing
emotional support animal,
but what if,
outside one day,
just working in the yard,
I have a horrible chainsaw accident
and die
and he (or she)
is in the house
maybe because I let her (or him) sleep in,
for example,
and no one finds my stupid, legless body for days
and he (or she)
is hungry
and frightened
and alone,
barking at my stupid, dead, legless body
from a window,
if I'm even within sight of a window;
Bark!
"Get up! Let me out!"
Bark bark!
"I need to pee! I want to play dead, too!"
Bark bark bark!
"Where's my ball? Are you lying on my ball?"
and in the meantime he (or she)
has to drink from the toilet?

I should get a dog,
but what if I became attached
and I *don't* have
a horrible chainsaw accident,
but one day he (or she)
seems a little off,
so we go to the vet
and the vet says,
"There's nothing I can do.
If only you'd brought her (or him) in yesterday
instead of working in your stupid yard."
and I have to put him (or her)
down
and stand there,
helpless yet again,
and watch her (or him)
die,
as I've stood and watched so many,
too many,
in my life
die,
leaving me more frightened
and alone,
even more broken,
grieving,
hungry for companionship,
which is why I got him (or her)
in the first place.
Then what would I do?
Get a dog?

Dreams

You can have too many dreams
and the ones that will break you
are the ones that come true.

Because when you lose them—
and you will—
lose them,

it will make shuffling arthritically
to the kitchen one morning,

before your spine thaws
and balance returns,

to discover there's just barely
a full cup of four-day-old coffee
waiting in the bottom of the pot

feel like winning
the goddamn Powerball.

Empathy for a Spider

The little spider in your shower's
labored many spidery hours
to move its web from the corner
where it long ago started
to a crack near the floor
where the grout's a bit parted.

This feckless little arachnid
in his reckless little snack bid
mistakes the crack for a hole,
from which he hopes may emerge
(mayhap, on the verge?)
some tasty, supper-like soul.

He fails to see with his spidery eyes
that his silly spider's enterprise
is a plan that just takes the cake,
as the crack's not a hole
it's a crack that,
on the whole,
is a hole that's really quite fake,

for your shower is clean,
a housekeeper's dream,
antiseptic and perfectly dry,
an improbable place
in any spider's case
for a spidery meal to draw nigh.

It's been parched the whole time,
nothing less than a crime,
abandoned since you departed,

stranding me here alone,
out of place in our home,
quite sad and so broken-hearted.

Like a spider, I hover
in the hope of a miracle,
nothing too grand or especially lyrical,
just for you to return
from your private sojourn
from wherever it is you've gone,
to sit and dine quietly,
just our spider, you, and me,
perhaps today, or anon.

Like my brother, the spider,
I'm a lost lover, not a fighter,
becalmed in this arid, empty space,
my hunger now pain,
nothing to gain,
no sustenance,
and certainly
no grace.

At sixes and sevens
the doorway to heaven
offers none who pass passage back,
the gateway to salvation
just another privation
and in truth,
for me,
just a crack.

Elephant in the Room

I didn't love her
because she was alive
to receive my love

or love her
because she was in my presence.

I loved her whether
she was lying next to me
or in another country,

when I could see her
and when I couldn't,
when I could talk to her,
hear her replies,

or when she was far out of range.

I loved her at all times,
in all places,
together or apart

and I love her still.

I can no more replace her now
than I could or would have
replaced her
when she was alive.

For me
she lives on,
present in every thought
even though out of sight,
silent,
beyond my horizon,

no longer here,
where the love remains.

Butterscotch

Tell me what butterscotch tastes like.
I'll wait.

//

In that same way,
I'll never tell you what I've lost.

Yes,
of course,
the sights, tastes, smells
and oh, god,
the sounds, the touch.

But nothing I'll say,
no words I can rivet to this page,
will ignite in you
what they burn in me.

She was butterscotch.

Möbius Trip

I stand at my printer as it spits out poems like it has a bad taste in its mouth, cleansing its palette with the paper and ink it takes to print a poem about how to think about thinking about standing at a printer writing a poem that's getting the best of me about standing at a printer as in some pointless Escher sketch of me standing at a printer thinking about writing a poem about watching verse issue forth as consciousness ricochets deep south to far north between what's real and what's not, what I had and what I've lost, what you paid and what it cost until what's real and what isn't is just as persistent as the ink on the paper, bloodless communion wafers still gushing from my printer as I rush back to my laptop, doggerel dithering lapdog, to capture these thoughts before they're lost in the fog of thinking about standing at my printer thinking about writing poems as it prints this frantic, phrenic lint, adding to the cost of living a life in paper and ink, thinking and giving a damn sight more for writing than living until I can't remember what I was thinking before I was standing at my printer watching it spit out these poems with a bad taste in my mouth.

Ghosts

It's been years now since you lived here
It won't be many more
before I leave our home as well

I don't plan to haunt the place
though I don't know
if that's my decision

I've never felt you haunted our home
at least not in the way
you haunt my thoughts

As for ghosts
I think mine is already here
just waiting his turn

The Greef

Shhhhh! Be quiet!
You'll wake the goddamn Greef!
No,
yeah,
I know,
I shouldn't have to live like this,
but just be careful,
wouldja?

When did I get it?
Well, my wife got sick
and it just started
showing up
and it was better than
nothing,
those scary nights alone,
not knowing,
and then she died
and it got bigger, like . . .

a *lot* bigger,
you know?
but it felt like
just then,
just for a little while,
we needed each other
and I thought
eventually
it would get sick of me
and leave

so I let it inside,
let it stay,
and now I know
that was my first mistake,
and then it just,
I don't know,
settled in,
took charge somehow
and now I can't . . .
I don't know how
to get rid of the damn thing.
There are days
I don't see it around as much.
I don't know where it goes
to hide
but I can feel it,
it's always there,
waiting
for just the wrong moment
to grab me, then
other days

I wake up
fresh into the nightmare
and there it is,
lying on my chest,
staring me right in the face
and it just hangs on
all day, then
settles down in bed
draped over my head.

Nothing I've tried
seems to discourage it,
and as much as I want
to be rid of it,
sometimes
the only thing that seems . . .
like it could be worse . . . ?
than living this way . . . ?
is not living this way.

The Visitor

Another trip
to your grave today,
nothing new to see,
even less to say,
only the thought
that there'll come a day
I'll arrive not to grieve,
but to stay.

going under

that night
the one you died
I went under
never to resurface

I live still
I don't know how
with no air
little light
no laughter

there are others
down here
I sense them
more than see them

but no matter
there is no company
in this misery

Time Heals

Time heals all wounds
is temporally idiotic,
as if time were some balm,
grief's antibiotic.

Time is only what we choose to believe,
a tablespoon of days
sipped from cradle to grave
until it's our turn to leave.

As for wounds,
some heal, some don't,
time no cure for those who grieve so,
no balm at all,
merely placebo.

Upside

Being dead has its advantages.
No more sunburns.
No tedious meetings, running long.
No goddamn performance reviews.
Finally losing that stubborn weight.
No more deductibles.
No need to exercise.
No more telemarketers.
Or politicians.
No ticks, no taxes.
No debt or jury duty.
No sitting in traffic
or waiting at the DMV.
No mowing. No weeds.
No babies on airplanes.
No computer viruses,
hackers, or haircuts.
No pain.
No self-doubt,
no additional regrets,
no grocery lists.
No more wondering
what it will be like to die.
No more weddings to attend
and just the one funeral.

Gravity

Four years
and I'm near forgetting
what it's like not to be alone.

No one to share the gravity
that pulls at me;
too much air for one person to breathe.

Silence
nurses old echoes,
trying to revive a noisier time.

The television makes conversation,
mocking, irrelevant;
I am mute in response.

As it recedes,
listless sunlight
leaves the darkness unedited.

What Do You Get the Woman Who Has Nothing?

It's the same every year now,
your birthday coming round again
and I don't know what to get you.

There's nothing you need and
I wouldn't know how to get it to you anyway.
Some new plantings might be nice

but it's a bit too early,
not quite Spring,
so there could still be a frost.

Perhaps a nice bench,
though I'm not sure if you can have one.
Still, it would be nice to have a place to sit

and talk with you,
remember the times
when we could both feel the sun,

a place to watch the birds
and listen for your voice in the wind
as it dries my tears.

As Morning Approaches

If you've watched
a honeyed autumn dawn
pour over Boston
from the eighth floor
of a hospital
as your love lies
in the bed behind you,
your shoulders quaking
with stifled tears
lest she wakes
to see what's in your eyes,
to know you believe
she's dying,
with nothing left to try
and you'll not share this season again,
you can learn to hate
fall's golden light
in memory and recurrence.

Grumpy Dog

I need a grumpy dog
I want a surly cat
or a pissed-off goldfish
that makes people say,
What's his problem?

I need a messy yard
I want a noisy truck
or a dumpster caught on fire
so the neighbors think,
What's his problem?

I need a fallen tree
I want a lawn of weeds
or an old fridge by the garage
so passersby ask,
What's his problem?

Without that grumpy dog
or messy yard
or fallen tree

without that surly cat
or noisy truck
or lawn of weeds

without that angry goldfish
or dumpster fire
or broke-ass fridge

who will say
or think to ask
Do you have a problem?

Winter

Winter's blue, beetled light
creeps quietly through the glass,
its tender, sullen bite

numbs the floors with frost,
chokes the fire in the hearth,
until all I know is cold,

embers burnt to rust,
life itself grown old,
blood clabbered in my veins

as death approaches
astride a stalking horse,
holding winter's icy reins.

My New Lover

I didn't choose her,
didn't plan for this to happen;
we met and—before I knew it—
she moved in and took over my routine.

She's not fond of laughter,
prefers me in tears, and
if I get any sleep at all,
it's always on her schedule.

The longer we're together
the more friends she alienates,
as she schemes to isolate me
from the world before.

I spend so much time with her
it's hard to think about much else,
or remember what life was like
before she began calling the shots.

People say we should break up,
that I should push her away, move on,
but it's not as simple as that
when grief takes you as a lover.

What Is This Place?

I have no context
in which to live without you,
no frame of reference,
reality only real to me
when you were here.
It's not that I deny
you're gone

or I don't know
that you're dead.
I *know* that.
I know that because
I've never hated
knowing something
more than I hate knowing that.

It's that my *expectation* of you,
like the expectation
of my next heartbeat,
is autonomic,
requiring neither thought nor effort,
and can't be un-known.

The only frequency I can hear
is tuned to your voice,
replaced now with white noise.
I no more expect not to see you
when I enter a room,
when I look out to the patio,

when I peek into your office
for the hundredth time today,
than I expect my blood
to turn to air in my veins,
the air I breathe
to turn bloody in my lungs.

My consciousness is
saturated with you,
axiomatic, unelidable,
the geography of my brain
a topographic record of
loving you.

It's not that I don't know you're dead,
I know that all too *fucking* well.
It's that there is no resetting that,
not in my hearing,
not in my vision,
not in my thoughts.

So I still hear you,
I still see and feel you,
still smell and taste you,
I still talk to you,
walk with you,
wait for you.
You inhabit me
as we inhabited one another
in another now.

And if I could
reboot, move on,
get over it,
get beyond it,
build a new life,
let you go,
allow time to heal this carnage,
make a new plan,
carry on—
who would I be then
except a broken me
with a missing you?
And how would that
be different from today?

Half a Loaf

If you need love
you may have mine.
I grant you,
it's well worn.
It got a lot of use
before she died.
I made sure
she was never without it.

Now it's old and bruised,
like that one banana
at the supermarket that
everyone passes up for
a newer, fresher one,
even one that's a little green.

Still,
maybe you could use it
to make a nice banana bread
that you could offer to
someone as special as she was.
What's that?
No . . . no.
My days in the kitchen are past.
I'd only make a mess.

Trees

What a thing.
The varieties,
the beauty.
Feeding us,
producing oxygen,
providing shelter,
raw materials,
home to so many species.
Essential.
No trees,
no us.

Yet,
all the dendrologists,
all the silvologists,
Theophrastus himself—
none can answer
the most fundamental question:

Why?
the question
at the marrow of everything,
haunts me now.
You were
sustenance,
air,
shelter,
my home.
Gone now.
Why?

I cannot imagine
surviving,
wanting to survive,
a world without trees.

Race Point Beach

There was that time
driving to the Cape
with Einstein,
the delightful but dim
little teddy bear
I surprised you with
to keep you company
in the hospital
while you recovered
from knee surgery,
bopping away on your lap
to "Caribbean Queen,"
that summer's hot song.

We went to P'Town
where you wanted to see
the tip of the Cape,
so we drove
to Race Point Beach
where you made your way
down the dunes
to the water
to breathe in the Atlantic
while ripples from Portugal
lapped at your good foot.

It was then
we discovered
how much easier
going down a dune
on one leg and crutches is
than going up,
so I carried you
up the liquid sand,
struggling to hold you
at arm's length
to not cause you pain,
your casted leg cradled
in the crook of an elbow.

That was when you knew
we'd make it,
that this fresh relationship
was going to thrive,
that it wasn't just
a playful dancing bear
that would entertain for
a summer
then melt into memory.

You're gone now,
I can only wish
to some lovely,
end of the world beach,
while Einstein waits,
the way teddy bears do,
for you to reappear.
He still loves that song,
but he doesn't dance anymore.

The Web We Weave

I spend so damn much time
wishing I were dead,
imagine what I could get done
if I wished for life instead.

Clean out all the closets,
finally sort out the garage,
tackle my messy workshop,
make my first collage,

paint the roof a lighter shade,
wax the driveway 'till it shines,
forge myself a duller blade,
pickle my soul in brine.

Instead, I sit here writing down
every hopeless thought,
the agony of the moth in a web
when it knows it's truly caught,

struggling and desperate,
full of self-reproach,
praying for a measure of mercy
as the spider plans its approach.

How Dare I?

Do you think
you can just kiss my nose
anytime you like?
she would say
each time I kissed her nose
and
because it was one of our games
and games have rules
I would say
pretty much
yeah
which was her cue to remind me
that she knew Judo
which indeed she did
but
due to the disparity in our sizes
and logarithmic difference
in relative strength
I would respond
well
you'd better know two or three
of his best friends
too
and we would laugh
and hug and
I would kiss her nose again
and sometimes
even again after that
and now I would exchange
whatever vacant life I have left
to kiss her nose

and have her upbraid me
just one last time
do you think
you can just kiss my nose
anytime you like?
her brow furrowed
in mock outrage
above her glittering,
laughing eyes.

Sunrise

just my luck
I woke up
to another day
not worth a sunrise

sand in my veins
moon in my eyes
losses in mind
drunk with time

unliving my life
beggared my wife
ruing the days
lost in this place

numb with grief
sick with pain
far too broken
to do it again

praying for night
where dreamless relief
darkens another day
not worth the sunrise

Hug Me

Life will never again
be so livable
so fully and happily
alive
as when it held you
as when I held you

warm and laughing
wrapped in a hug
that delighted and
deliciously frightened you
knowing

that I controlled its ardor
like a friendly boa
that would always
always
release you on command
but still . . .

If I'd Been Your Dog

If I'd been your dog
of course I'd miss you,
but I wouldn't understand
you won't be back.

I'd still look for you every day
with happy anticipation,
believing
there's a chance you'll appear,
if not later,
probably tomorrow.

In the meantime,
I'd still enjoy my supper,
the thrilling toss of a ball,
the noise and light
from the box on the wall and
in time,
who really knows,

I might not miss you
that much at all,
or not so much
it would spoil a good walk
or trouble a pleasant nap.

All I'd require is
the occasional pat,
a scratch behind my ears,
to help me remember
not to forget
and spare me human tears.

I Am

broken—
in a way that survives repair

sad—
as a way of life

penitent—
for sins I'm unaware I committed

mute—
screaming from this page for relief

tired—
of always getting my way

bored—
with cloned days that turn to years

spent—
heart beating out of biological habit

grateful—
for everything but this

stunned—
by the endurance of grief

remodeled—
as a single need that cannot be met

lonely—
but only for her

If I Were a Dog

If I were a dog
I could hope
some kind person
might notice me,
lost and hopeless,
and pick me up off the street,
perhaps offer me some water
or a bit of their sandwich,

then take me to a shelter, where
after a gentle exam,
maybe even a warm bath
and a pleasant towel dry,
the Vet might take pity
on this tired, good boy
and relieve me of my misery.

Sadly,
I am not a dog.

If I Had Been Your Cat

Somebody died?
Oh, great.
NOW who's going to feed me?
Christ, it's always something.
By the way,
that box?
The one I crap in?
It's not gonna empty itself.

Smoke and Mirrors

Standing at the hall closet
I breathe the telltale musk
of long-extinguished flames
and smoke finer than memory
still insinuating
the canvas work coat I wore
as we tended the bonfire.

Past burning, past caring,
I close my eyes,
bathe in the scent of memory,
red-orange fingers flicking the air,
whipcrack of expanding branches
exploding,
cautious darkness ringing us in,
cool meadow air at our backs,
faces fever-painted
as our bodies court the vortex
to surround us.

I burn for the heat
of that long-dead fire,
you beside me,
holding hands in our hushed,
end-of-the-world crucible,
melted by the beckoning flames,
the gentle pressure of your touch,
breathing your smoke,
warmed by your fire,
exalted by the night air
and the screak of a wary owl.

Kiss It Better

All this writing
a cry for attention,
a child's plea
for adult intervention,
to hug it away,
say it's OK,
make it not real,
kiss it better,

clean out the wound,
apply disinfectant,
add a Snoopy bandage
and leave me expectant
of a better day tomorrow,
possibly ice cream tonight,
but please,
won't someone just say
it will all be OK,
and make everything all right?

My Ghost

My ghost slept by my side
endless, blank years—

all of time.

Then I woke,
lived a life without him—

and he missed me.

I loved, was loved in return,
now I grieve—

and he wants to feel that for himself.

My ghost is hungry now
and in my electric sleep, he dreams—

dreams of replacing me.

Simple Pleasures

I'd like to go with you
to the beach
just one more time,
see you across a room
and think
"She's mine,"

ask if you'd like
to go for a ride
and while you get ready,
just wait outside.

I want to carry the groceries
in from your car
and when you wake for the day
ask how you are,

hear you gasp with delight
at tomorrow's sunrise,
then surprise you with chocolate
for the look in your eyes.

I want to lie in our bed
and listen to you breathe,
find a way to stop crying,
a more arid way to grieve.

I want to stop writing these poems
because I don't need to
after finding a way
to go on dying without you.

Sandy

The day you died,
twenty-five years ago today,
we sat with you in silence,
Dennis and I,
as we had for days,
the only sound
the quiet of your labored breathing.

Thoughts like the Boston sky,
cloudy, gray,
we waited, hung fire,
younger brother,
older brother,
middle sister,
three siblings ill-fated to be two.

Death eased into the room,
as the nurse
who had sat with you through the day,
attending to your needs
and our agony,
rose to leave,
her shift come to an end.

She stood over you
and whispered what an honor
it had been to know you,
serve you,
and at the moment she bent down
and unexpectedly kissed your forehead
to bid her goodbye,
a tentative gap opened in the clouds.

Amber end-of-day light
suffused the room
as you exhaled your life's summary breath,

your permission to leave
granted by a kiss,
your path now clear in the honeyed light,
your brothers,
not ready for you to go,
there to say goodbye
and cling to each other in desperation.

Christmas 2021

I didn't set out
to be this person.

I never expected
to end up like this,
alone,
lonely,
my love living
in a graveyard
a few minutes,
incalculable distance,
from our home.

I never expected
my siblings would die
before me,
or that I,
youngest child
by a wide margin,
would become
the older brother.

I see now
it's not about
the setting out
or expectations,
illusions
that divert us from
the randomness,
like the tornado that spares
that one house,

or the butterfly-wing
shit luck
that deposits some,
ascendant,
at flag-whipped peaks
while others tumble
unarrested
into an unavoidable
crevasse,

a crack in the ice
that could have been
named for us
years ago
when we believed
we were free agents,
making our own decisions,

charting our own course,
now living Christmas
in our solitary, icy cave,
frostbitten,
straining
for the distant echo
of our lover's voice.

No Upside

I don't want to drink milk from the bottle anymore,
or when I undress, toss my clothes on the floor.

I want to do all your errands when I'm out doing my own
and surprise you with the news when I return home.

I don't want to make a mess now and clean it up sometime,
or flip through the channels until way past our bedtime.

I'm sick of climbing the stairs to go to bed on my own,
knowing it won't be you when I answer the phone.

I'd like to make a meal that takes more than a minute,
bake you a casserole and have you ask me what's in it.

I'm tired of spending pointless days alone,
returning to our house without bringing you home.

I don't want to dream without you to share,
or learn how to pray now I don't have a prayer.

Salvation

Offered the chance to become immortal
I'd sooner seek the nearest portal,
and I can only hope that reincarnation
is just another thoughtless creation.

Once around this merry-go-round
has proved enough for me,
the thought of eternity in this eternal pain?
Well, let's just let that be.

No, "forever" holds the same appeal
as a steaming glass of vinegar,
the recipe derived from wine or apples,
but the outcome far more sinister.

Sentenced to await the world's destruction
is less a blessing, more an abduction,
held in a castle by unseen captors,
confined without rope, but plenty of rafters,

so let the chips fall wherever they may
when I reach that blessed dying day,
let whatever happens next, or not,
happen as it will,
just no more, I beg you,
of this bitter, biting pill,

and if there's no heaven, then so be it,
and let that be a lesson to all of the theists,
or if existence smolders down to a fiery hell,
well, that would burn nearly as well,

but if I simply rise to another day,
the seed of billions to the end of time,
my first stop will be my local precinct
to allege and confess the perfect crime,
the act and sentence one and the same,
never allowed to exit the game.

Last Rites

The condemned
get a last meal,
a chance to speak,
both duly noted,
minutiae of the state.

As I woke today,
thoughts of you circulating
like blood,
it came to me,
sadly,
that I can't say
what your last meal was,
or what your last words were.

There just came a time
when you no longer could eat,
and a moment when
the drug that allowed you
to escape the pain
wouldn't permit you to awaken
one last time

to say "I love you," or
"What day is it?" or
"Am I OK?" or
"I love you."

and I didn't know at either of those moments
though I was with you
every hour of every day to the last
that those moments had come and gone.

Why didn't someone tell me,
warn me,
that was how it would be,
so I could record such meaningless things?

We do that for the people we kill,
it seems only fitting
that we would do that for
those we love.

Roommates

You don't learn to live
with Death—
Death lives with *you*.

It doesn't care
what's for dinner,
or what's on TV.

Death doesn't put its feet up on the furniture,
leave a mess in the bathroom,
or hog the covers.

It doesn't have annoying friends over,
read your journal,
or eat the last of the lasagna.

Death is simply—*present*—
always—
wherever you try to be,

to remind you,
should you ever suffer a moment's peace,
just what you've lost.

Ashes to Ashes

Understand
you are not dead
but always dying,
perhaps
a breath or two,
heartbeat or ten
distant from
denouement,
final scene nothing
as you'd imagined it;
peaceful,
farewells in place,
job well-done,
life well-lived,
affairs tidy and neat,
precious one
stroking hand or hair.

Instead,
disarray and
unrequited e-mail,
unbalanced laundry in the washer,
bed unmade,
bills unpaid,
taxes due,
cellphone buzzing,
pan on the stove
soon to boil dry,
subsequent fire
a fitting inferno,
legacy consumed,

alone on the
cold, hard
bathroom floor,
intestate,
soul agape,
temperature rising,
dog scratching
at the door,
smoke in your eyes.

Reconciled

No more question
whose toothbrush is whose,
or easy discussions
of which movie to choose.

When I simply can't find it,
I'm alone as I prospect
and I'm not sure who bought that,
but there's no other suspect.

No need to hang up my jackets
or hide boots and shoes,
no more heads, you win,
tails, I gracefully lose.

It's always clear now
who left the garage open,
and if I feel like some popcorn,
it's no use just hoping.

It's up to me now
to make up the bed
and do my own cooking
if I want to get fed.

Just one more time
I wish you'd hog the whole blanket,
there'd be no protest from me
at this beggar's lone banquet.

So much has changed
and none of it good,
if there's a price I could pay,
I'd pay it in blood,

but life's outcomes are final,
we arrive where we're led,
whether desperately alive,
or quietly dead.

Dead End

I feel nothing
as acutely as I once did.
In the end
pain is no more sustainable
than life.

The primal ache
of your death
treads neural pathways
enervated by overuse,

the trail leading
from nowhere to nothing,
looping and crossing itself
in an endless tangle,

a Möbius strip of endless grief,
no top or bottom,
one cliff's edge,
the beginning of the end

ending where it begins,
a labyrinth of lost hope and regret,
memories always underfoot,
your ghost always just ahead,
out of reach.

Inside Voice

I live inside your shadow,
splintered, dark, and hollow,
life in black and white,
surviving since you died
on expired air,
stale regret,
and the many tears I've cried.

I'd wed your shadow if I could,
merge my eidolon with your own,
escape this earthly station
to endure your shattered world
as we importuned the universe
to impeach this devastation.

Piglets

The other wives at our table
on that pointless corporate cruise,
dutifully appointed in their
duty-free, island-gold
necklaces, earrings, and bracelets,
asked you,
*(whom they foolishly considered
their private Cinderella)*
if *you* had bought anything,
(poor dear)
and with no hint of self-consciousness,
you gestured towards your neck and ears,
where they noticed for the first time
and squealed in unguarded delight,
Oh my God!
Are those crystal PIGLETS?
suddenly dissatisfied
as they witnessed
through gold-shuttered lives
the simple contentment in your eyes,
the glittering love in mine,
their auspicious conformity
melting in the face of your
modest, humorous
and stunningly personal
accessorizing.

Brainiac

All the hippos in my hippocampus
matriculate to the latest dances,

and while their bulk is no light matter
they tread quite lightly on my white matter,

careful to avoid creating craters
as they chassé across the dura mater,

dreaming of my lateral ventricles
when snug inside their sleeping tent-acles,

while all the mooses in my hypothalamus
eschew the hippo's terpsichorean fuss

and in lieu of dancing, amble and scatter
amidst the folds of my graying gray matter,

browsing for butterflies, hunting for honeybees
amidst sad neurons derailed by Wernicke's,

dreaming of an extended vacation
far from the ungodly devastation

your death has wrought in my temporal lobes,
cremating all my dreams and hopes

Picture Perfect

I have this picture,
the one I took that day
we set out to get your hero shot.

The sky,
gently overcast,
served up just the right light,
exposing all the details,
nothing washed out,
tentative, milky shadows
in counterpoint.

The background
nothing but creamy snow
as I shot from below,
looking up at you
high on the slope,
slight compression of
perspective from the
telephoto.

You in your chili-red,
one-piece snowsuit,
black accents
offset by white and black gloves,
contrasting white hat,
whipped cream topping
on that beautiful Sunday,

in the middle of a perfect turn
to skier's left
on a steep blue slope,
skis railed to their edges,
perfect spray pattern from the
frozen powder
radiating tip to tail,
every inch engaged,
skis matched—

no, more than matched—
perfectly parallel,
exactly hip-width apart,
one knee nestled
into the other and
angled to the slope,
razor edges carving
an arc into the frozen surface,
driving you to the next transition,

lower-body crossing the hill,
upper-body
tall and in the fall-line,
arms extended,
reaching down,
poles in perfect position,
releasing the last turn,
anticipating the next,

nothing in your form
open to criticism,
even your smile
perfect,
as you knew
in that moment
nothing could feel better than
this,
than overcoming everything
you ever had to face
and still be able to do
this—

not OK,
not well,
not even better than most
(though you never cared about that)
but perfectly,
a moment in a lifetime,
a lifetime in a moment,
wordless, active joy personified,
your love of your world,
your life,
frozen,
on full display.

This is what I see
every night
before the light goes out
and every morning
as I open my eyes
to watch you
ski down our bedroom wall.

In the Moment

Most moments
are exactly that,
but not the one
I met you
and not the one
you died,
two moments that,
together,
set the course of my life,
then ended it.

The years between
came and went,
carelessly spent,
in what, I swear,
was just a moment.
Now
there's only one remaining
that might matter
to anyone,
if not to me.

Of Red Queens and Rabbit Holes

I can't escape the rabbit hole,
I'm the rabbit and rabbit hole both,
the Red Queen's leavened riddle,
answered with half a loaf.
I'm what ends up giving
when I give it all I've got,
I'm the buzzer and the ball
as I miss the three-point shot,
the killer and the sitter
in the horror movie trope,
the prisoner at his hanging,
as well as the hangman's rope.

Beset by wicked witches,
it's I who's the wickedest witch,
I'm what occurred to myself
at the infamous Owl Creek bridge,
the one who can't stop catching
the grief I've already caught,
the fool who keeps on thinking
his dreary, foolish thoughts,
the lost and lonely visage
at your wretched, hopeless grave,
the one who couldn't save you
with no hope of being saved

No Choice

As if it were possible
the exhausted blankness I felt today
was worse than the pain
it supplanted.
If those are my choices,

I'll have the pain back again.
The agony
at least acknowledges you
while it consumes me
one memory at a time.

Bent

Every hangman's rope
has a beginning at each end.

Exits round the curve
in the middle of the bend.

Up can be down
when there's no one around,

and lost just a way
to say something's unfound.

Every life has a death
at the start and conclusion,

full of curves, twisted and bent,
completing the illusion.

Up can't exist without going down
roads full of curves, all begun but confounded

by the lives and deaths, twisted and bent,
by the pain that they surrounded.

Memento Mori

I have my mother's teeth,
yellowed like the ivory keys
of an old piano,
the kind people offer for free
in the hope that someone
will look past the obvious defects
and haul the carcass away,

keys mottled and stained
by time and hesitant, oily fingers
caressing a melody,
nothing like the blazing white
veneers and implants so popular today,
dentures fit for angels,
snow-blinding smiles
that do not occur in nature.

Perhaps,
had I been born
into circumstances where
such things as braces
and unnaturally white teeth
weren't considered
something only attainable by those
of a higher caste,
perhaps then
I'd have a winning smile,
flashing like a lighthouse,
beguiling the unwary,
slowly drawing them near,
until I could wreck them on
the reefs and shoals of these words.

Leaving Home

Each time I leave
what was our home
I've no expectation I'll return
because everyone dies,
as you did,
and there's nothing
to forestall that same stalking terror
from surprising me while I'm out.

So
I start the dishwasher,
kill the water to the washing machine,
ensure the toilets are flushed,
tell Siri to turn off the music
I play nearly round the clock
to quell the relentless, joyful,
acid memories
that fuel my thoughts,

because
who needs to come behind me
to blaring music,
ants parading over dirty dishes,
fermenting toilets,
and a house flooded by a failed hose,
all signs that I foolishly believed
the last threshold I'd cross
would be my own?

Irreplaceable

I am sorry,
so sorry
to have not let this go.
I know that's inconvenient,
awkward at best.
It's just that
no matter where I turn,
she is there.
Not as a ghost, no,
nothing so substantial,
but as wish,
memory,
thought,
desire;
pain.

Please;
do not
suggest I move on,
an idea I find
viscerally repellent.
Don't tell me
she would want me to be happy,
the assumption close
behind the notion
of finding her replacement.

She is not subject to
replacement,
just as a missing
limb
can't be replaced with
anything more than
an animated facsimile
that causes onlookers
to think,
"How hard that must be."

I haven't lost
a childhood teddy
or beloved pet
that can be substituted,
affections transferred
to a new host,
past life dimmed
in remembrance,
like the red-rimmed sun still
raging behind the smoke of a forest fire.

And I am so sorry
that my situation
may insist you consider
what may await you,
your own trial.
That much,
at least,
is not my fault.

Crossword

Christ in a sidecar,
even the morning crossword
conspires to bring you to mind
with the clue:
Pixar movie in the top ten of the 2000s,
the answer one of your favorites,
solely for the scene of the little robot
organizing his trailer,
sorting his precious junk,
thrilling you to your very marrow,
as you loved to sort and decide,
organize and reorganize,
and especially discard,
so here I sit,
unintended throwaway,
crossword ambush victim
in tears again,
quiet morning reorganized
by the memory of your animated delight.

Ice

There was ice that day, too,
three years ago,
when I was desperate to meet you at the church,
ice barring me from getting down our driveway,
until the panicked call to our plow guy,
explaining the situation through rising tears,
that your funeral was in half an hour
and the ice had me trapped.

I hadn't finished choking out the story
before he said,
"I'm on it." and hung up.
In less than five minutes, he appeared,
the driveway got sanded
and I made it to the church with your sisters,
just a few minutes behind you.

The ice this day wasn't quite enough
to leave me stuck at home.
There was no funeral this year,
so I stood outside the closed and locked church,
just as lost, confused,
just as compelled
as the non-migratory geese barking overhead,
to make this journey.

One of the neighbors appeared,
slipping and sliding on the sidewalk,
dragged along by their dog on his leash,
hot on the trail of just the right spot
to relieve himself,
the household cat prancing cheerfully behind,
thinking, no doubt,
"What an idiot."

I watch this family circus until
everyone goes back inside.
From here, I'll follow the route
you traveled to the graveyard
on my annual pilgrimage
to visit the stations of your cross,
dragging my sins behind me,
leashed to this unsatisfying ritual,
thinking, "What an idiot."

Ghost

If you're a ghost to me
am I alive to you?
Or am I the ghost in this picture
from your ghostly point of view?

This is what ghosts must feel,
no point in the future,
no joy in the living,
all past, no posthumous,
more needing than giving.

I close my ghostly eyes and
this shadow-world disappears;
open them again
to find that I'm still here,

living a life I don't understand,
no longer comprehend,
ghosted heart gone with you,
wishing I was your ghost there, too.

Free Solo

I can write one verse
or a thousand,
cry to one person
or ten thousand
in search of solace.
Nothing changes.

I will always be alone
with your death.
No one can carry it for me,
experience it in my stead
or grant me relief,
even for just a while.
Your death is mine
alone
for the balance of my life.

Certainly, others grieve you,
but their grief is for them,
as mine is for me.
That is the essence of self.

We may
briefly
expose our pain to one another,
find some intimacy
in our adjacent wretchedness,
but will always part
with our burdens intact,
even if amended.

When I die,
my grief will pass to no one.
It will die with me
or accompany me.
This is revelatory,
even as it has no meaning for you.
Like my grief,
this certainty is mine
alone.

What She Doesn't Understand

"Open your heart once again,"
she said,
but my heart isn't closed,
it's simply taken,
claimed,
as it has always been
from the day you showed
me what your love was worth,
long before I would understand the cost.

"She wants you to be happy,"
she said,
but I am happy—
happy to have been in
her life for so many years,
happy to have loved
and been loved
beyond measure,
beyond sickness,
beyond death,
beyond grief.

My weeping is
equal parts pain
and gratitude
for the gift of knowing,
sitting here,
heart open,
joyful tears anointing my face,
that you were happy
to choose my heart
and grace it with a love
that grief will never displace
and none need ever replace,
as I pay the cost in sadness.

Enough Said

You might say,
"It's time to move on."
and I might say,
"To what?"

You might say,
"She'd want you to be happy."
and I might say,
"Not without her."

You might say,
"So, I have this friend . . ."
and I might say,
"No."

You might say,
"Why don't you just . . ."
and I might say,
"No."

You might say,
"I give up."
and I might say,
"It's time to move on."

Next

I don't want to learn how you carry your ghost
or let you see how I carry mine.

I don't want to put away her pictures
or empty her closet to make room for you.

I don't want to meet your relatives
or merge with your family before me.

I don't want to meet your friends,
be the living symbol of your progress.

I don't want to move
or expect that you'll move.

I don't want to make room for your car
by selling hers

or learn what makes you cry
by making you cry.

I don't want to watch
as you rearrange her kitchen.

I don't want to awaken and,
confusing you with her,

feel the momentary flood of relief,
followed by the pain rushing in again.

I don't want to see it in your eyes
when you realize this was a mistake.

I don't want to argue about it
or fight for some imagined us.

I don't want to help you pack
or wish you well

as you load your car
and drive back to your old life,

so I'll just say goodbye now,
before we ever say hello.

Fixer

I'm a fixer,
sliding or slotted into the role
by inclination and anxiety
over my siblings,
older brother and sister
fighting,
cat v. dog,
me so much younger,
surprising middle-age baby,
I didn't understand the inevitability
or naturalness of it,
knew only
it frightened me,
I hated it,
wanted desperately
to make it better,
make it stop.
Fix it.

So I patiently,
unconsciously,
assembled the tools
to become a repairman,
jester,
mediator,
arbitrator,
charting my career
and steering my relationships,
the first criteria for any partner
that they be broken in some way

that I would try
and frequently fail,
to fix,
because people often don't cotton
to unsolicited repairs.

Fixers often need fixing, too,
our own brokenness
disguised behind a dust-cloud
of compulsive rehabilitation,
so when we coupled,
two fixers discovering
their penultimate project,
you went to work
and I went to work
and we both healed
more than we could have alone
or in another's workshop,

until one day you broke
in a way I couldn't fix,
no one and nothing
could fix,
and as you tumbled
further and further
into dire disrepair,
my inadequacy ever more apparent,
our world was disassembled,
left in pieces
broken and dead,
living and broken.

Customer Service

"You have reached
1-800-Ask-God.
Your call is very important to us.
Please hold for the next representative."

(two years of silence)

"We're sorry.
All representatives are still busy
with other callers.
You are caller number :

108,070,001,948*

in the queue."

"Your expected wait time is:

4 millennia.

If you'd like
to receive a callback
from the next available representative,
please press:
9
followed by the pound key."

"If you prefer to hold,
please press:
1
followed by the pound key
for silence,"

"or press:
2
followed by the pound key,
for light jazz."

It is estimated that approximately 108 billion of our species has ever lived on Earth.

Photons

The light illuminating your lover's face
was born at a time when humans,
people we would recognize today,
were just emerging on earth.

Spawned in the core of the Sun,
the very definition of hell,
photons require 100,000 years
to careen some 433,000 miles
to the surface of our star

where they escape
at the speed of light,
earthbound,
to arrive a mere eight minutes later,

perhaps to illuminate a pane of stained glass
for blurred, penitent eyes;
possibly cause a child to squint
as they study the clouds for dinosaur shapes,

or just plunge heedlessly into the ocean,
diving as much as 1,000 meters,
below which
even light cannot hold its breath.

Obituary

Fate sealed,
passage booked,
I had no choice but to enter this world
and soon,
very soon,
I will have no choice but to leave it,
understanding no more about where I'm going
than where I emerged from,
or if, indeed,
there's a "where" in any piece of this.

I could proffer a list
of things I'll miss
but in truth,
I won't miss a damn thing,
any more than I miss anything before now,
as I have no memory of then,
so why should I expect memory of this?

So that leaves me here,
like a cardiac patient after surgery,
no recall,
only scars
to prove anything happened at all,
much of it taking place
while I slept
and others did what they could
to care for my faltering heart
as I prepare to depart once more.

Closure

The dead get closure
as nature's consolation prize
for dying.
For the living
it's something to hope for,
puzzle over,
less comprehensible
than infinity,
if you're not a physicist
or mathematician,
and I honestly believe
they're just kidding themselves.

Achieving closure
is like trying to grab hold
of a furious, wet cat.
There might be a moment
amidst the pain,
desperation,
and howling
when it seems possible,
only to end up
clawed, bloody, and shaken,
regretting the attempt
as the cat tears off,
even more wary of capture.

Beyond Imagining

I'm compelled to imagine you
into my world each day,

gently arranging parts and pieces
on a scaffold of memory.

The scent from your closet,
a faded note from your piano.

Watering your flowers at daybreak,
knowing your pleasure when you wake
to find the job done.

Driving your car, top-down, careful
not to glance over to the passenger seat.

Making up your side of the bed,
where it appears you had another restless night,

until I can nearly believe
you must be somewhere close by,

perhaps downstairs,
in the kitchen, getting coffee,

momentarily out of sight,
just beyond my hearing,

our paths about to cross for the first time today
only a moment from now,

because,
though I'm drowning in them,

what I cannot imagine
is another day without you.

Sundays

Sundays loom now
with the predictability
of a cold sore
and just as enjoyable.

In time past
one of us would wake
then wait contentedly
to welcome the other
to an unexplored day
mellow with possibility,
curious as new puppies.

I might deposit you at church
then go fetch breakfast donuts
while you found absolution,
each of us ensuring
there was enough for both,
then spend the day together

or just adjacent,
content with our activities,
the occasional glimpse and smile,
knowing the tides of the day
would soon enough see us
hand-in-hand
on the same shore.

Now your grave
stands like a lighthouse;
stern, immobile,
signaling monotony,
less warning than prophecy,

luring me to your final beach
where we'll share the sand again one day,
or perhaps just perpetual darkness,
each of us unaware of what came before
or the impending doom of the stars
that once illuminated our path.

Silence

The silence,
thick as cold syrup,
heavy as an executioner's soul,
hurts.

When you were here
you couldn't be so quiet
that I couldn't hear you,
hear
the vibration of your heartbeat
humming through the floorboards,
draw comfort from your every sigh.

Now the silence is alive
and it is restless,
ravenous,
insatiable,
consuming my senses.

It refuses to be banished by
my occasional voice,
non-stop music,
sad TV,
my wailing.

It inhales all these sounds
and returns
nothing,
the echo of death.

Plane Crash

Like a dog in a plane crash,
I have no idea what's going on.

Like a turtle on a fence post,
I don't know how I got here.

Like a cat in a parade,
I suppose this must be about me.

Like a blind man with a saw,
I only cut what I can't see.

Like a leech on a turnip,
I'm not getting what I need.

Like a pig at a barbecue,
I just want a chance to leave.

Appointed

An infinite line
less a single point
becomes two lines,
disappointing infinity.

An infinite life
less its singular point
marks a single void,
absolved of divinity.

Any point in a line
can be disappointed,
any point in a life
reappointed to joyless,

a search for relief
in a finite life
of pivotal points
all pointing to pointless.

The Problem

Omnipotence is a trap—
it forgives nothing,
while its possessor can forgive *anything*—
any wrong righted,
sin forgiven,
error corrected,
death avoided.

All it takes is a thought,
a wish, an impulse,
perhaps just a bit of omnipotent code,
an infinite if-then-else loop:
IF there's a problem;
THEN fix it;
ELSE do nothing;
END IF all problems solved.

Yet, in all of time,
other than home runs
and touchdowns
and the random trailer spared
from the odd tornado—
no rhyme, no reason,
no explanation,
for our chaos and unspeakable pain.

Oh, but the plan cannot be revealed
because you wouldn't understand!

And there's the trap:
It's *omnipotence*—
the ability to do *anything*—
put platypuses at the top of the food chain,
make jellyfish delicious,
double the speed of light,
create a somewhat less venal politician—

even grant us the capability to understand
this grand, mysterious,
oh-so-secret plan
of a trillion billion parts
and a billion trillion years,
so it simply begs the question:

What is God hiding?

The Silence

Silence inhabits me,
soft as time, patient
as a Monday church.

Its liquid pall
quenches the light,
mutes the clock.

Even the air
stirs cautiously,
hazards no sound,

lest the silence
escape my lungs
in a scream.

Pyhhric Victory II

Those last few days;
I've no way of knowing
if you knew,
but I was there
every moment,
determined
that Death,
when it came,
would not find you
without me,
have no chance
to think,
"Ahh, this one waits for me
alone,
unbeloved,"
and so it was
I had my Pyhhric victory
when our nightmare
became mine alone.

Rain

I want it to rain.

I want it to rain
like the sky has died
and the clouds can't hold back their tears.

I want it to rain
like time is on fire
and history has begun to smolder.

I want it to rain
until the air tumbles down
like a waterfall.

I want it to rain
until the blind can see
and the sighted go blind,

until I'm drowning in my bed,
carried away by torrents of you.

Sinner

I sat in the old church today,
the one we buried you from,
hoping to feel something—
anything—

other than loss,
the exhaustion of grief,
but nothing arrived
to take its place.

It was the hour of confession
and a dusting of penitents
alighted in the nave
to await their turn in the box.

One woman,
silver-haired and spry,
was in and out in far less than a minute
and I wondered how that was possible.

I'm not Catholic—not anything—
yet I expect I committed more sins
merely sitting there, writing,
than I could confess in thirty seconds.

Just the desire for relief,
for the white noise of faith
to suffocate my sorrow,
is likely a blasphemy of some sort.

Yet I left this space you found so sacred
unanointed, disbelieving,
my sins gathered about me,
grief's noose still tight around my neck.

What I Loved

I loved
making her laugh.

I loved
seeing her smile.

I loved
surprising her,
taking care of her.

I hate
that I've no chance to die
doing what I loved.

Motive Force

In the dream
we stayed downtown overnight
and came out in the morning
to our beat-up little truck,
all our stuff in the open bed,
to begin the short drive home.

We had to stop
after being blocked
by an empty firetruck.
I got out
to see what was wrong,
and it was then I saw
the hood was missing,
the battery, engine and
transmission all stolen
in the night.

We'd been driving
on the sheer belief
that we could,
but once we knew the truth
our little truck
no longer had reason to run,
so we started walking home.

In my living nightmare
I sleep alone each night.
One morning,
when I wake
and finally understand
you're gone,
my belief stolen,
perhaps I'll stop running
and begin the long walk home.

Roll Credits

My god, what a movie.

It felt so real,
like I was a character in it.

You came in a bit late
and had to leave early,

but you didn't miss
anything worth watching.

The theater's empty now
and the lights are going down.

Honestly, I'm a bit worn out
from the whole experience.

I might just rest here a while,
perhaps until the credits are finished.

Then I'll follow you.

Vigil

I sat
at the bedside
of my sister
as the sun
rent the clouds
and her soul fled
in the clotted light

I sat
at the bedside
of my mother
as her breathing
imperceptibly slowed,
until the interval
became infinite

I sat
at the bedside
of my father
as his radiant heart
froze,
his features creased
by a summary bolt of pain

I sat
at the bedside
of my wife,
breathless as she slept,
narcotized against the panic
of living her deepest fear
come to claim her

Now I sit,
last pawn
in a dark plan
yet unseen,
with no one to sit beside me

Supernova

I'm not struggling.
This is just who I am now,
no more or less authentic
but far less whole,
far less complete,
deeply unhappy.

I no longer fear
a future where she is ill
or in pain or dying
because we already visited
that particular hell,
though only one of us returned.

All that remains
is the last act
and I wait for it,
welcome it,
the way a star,
spent and exhausted,
welcomes going supernova.

It will be amazing
to just let go.

Epilogue

What's left
is merely epilogue,
dregs of last act tragedy
neither epigram nor homily.

How did he die?
How long did it take?
Did he suffer?
Was there anyone at the funeral?

Did he ever recover
from the loss of his lover?
Who got the house?
Did he ever get a dog?

About the Author

G. Greene is a late-to-the-game poet, born, raised, and now wrapping up his existence in a small town that calls itself a city in Western Massachusetts.

His earliest work, written as a child, was a simple rhyming poem commemorating the retirement of his elementary school Custodian, Mr. Stoddard. The note of thanks he received in return remains a treasured keepsake.

A Psychology major/English minor in college, later receiving an MBA degree, he has always, if somewhat sporadically, been a writer, even though the majority of his writing was in support of business proposals and marketing materials in his career as an executive manager, and later, a self-employed small-business consultant.

He met his incredible, accomplished wife, Jean M. Fielding, when they worked for the same aerospace and industrial hose company, before she resigned to pursue a degree in the law and then a 2nd career as a highly regarded criminal appellate attorney.

The loss of his wife in 2018 started his true journey as a sad poet.